Notebook

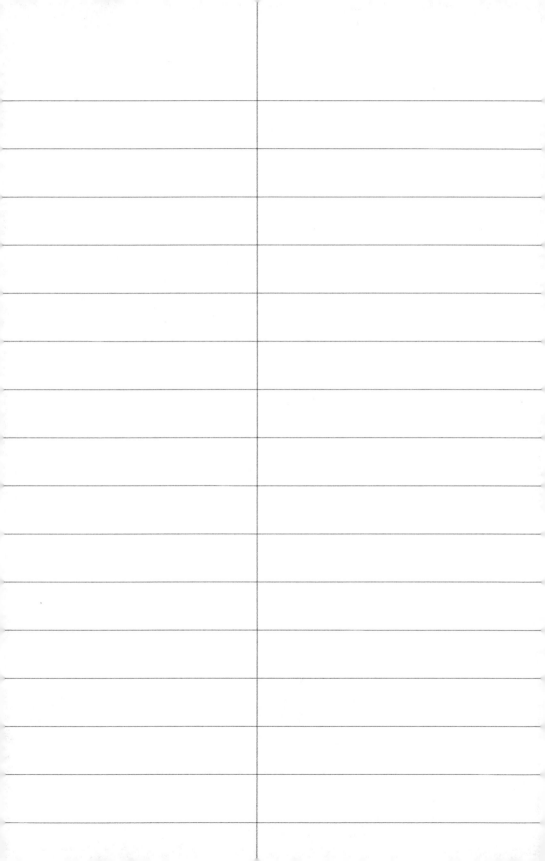

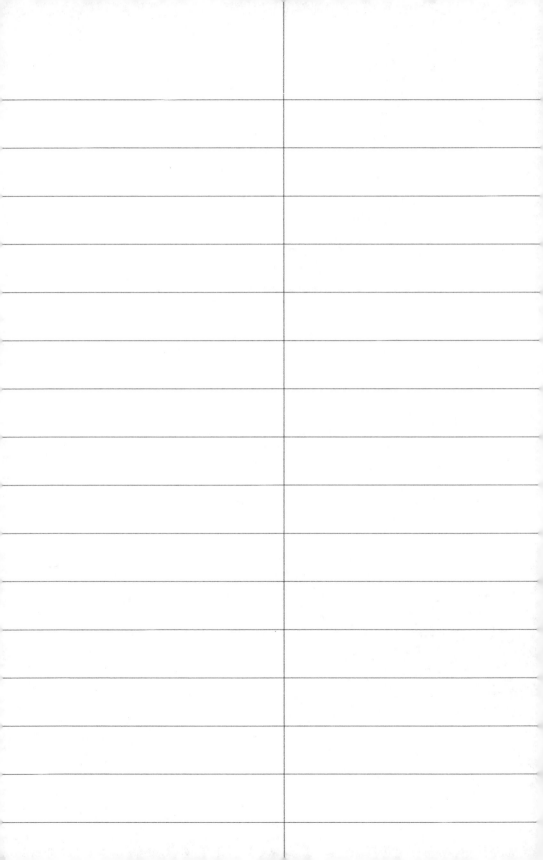

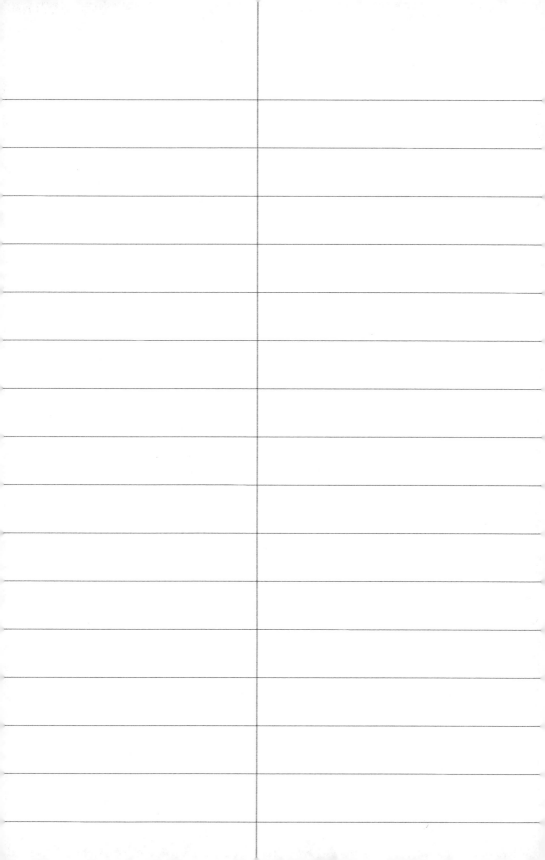

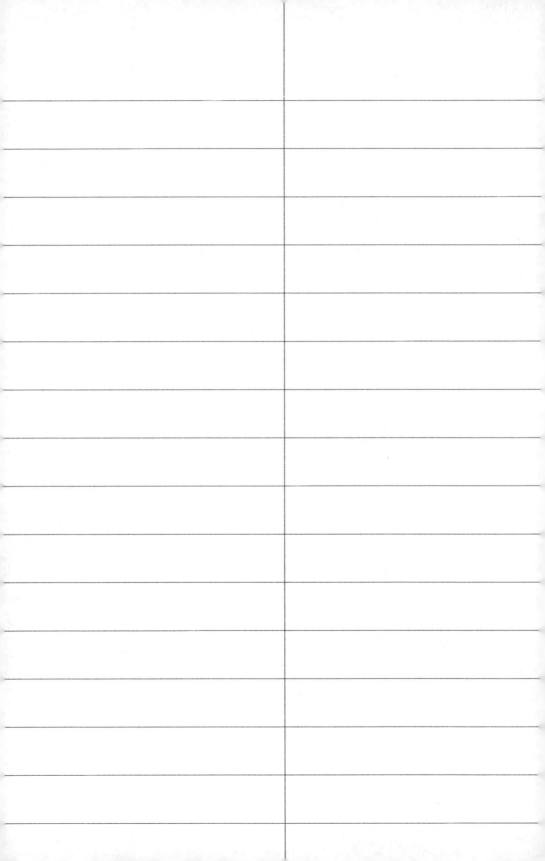

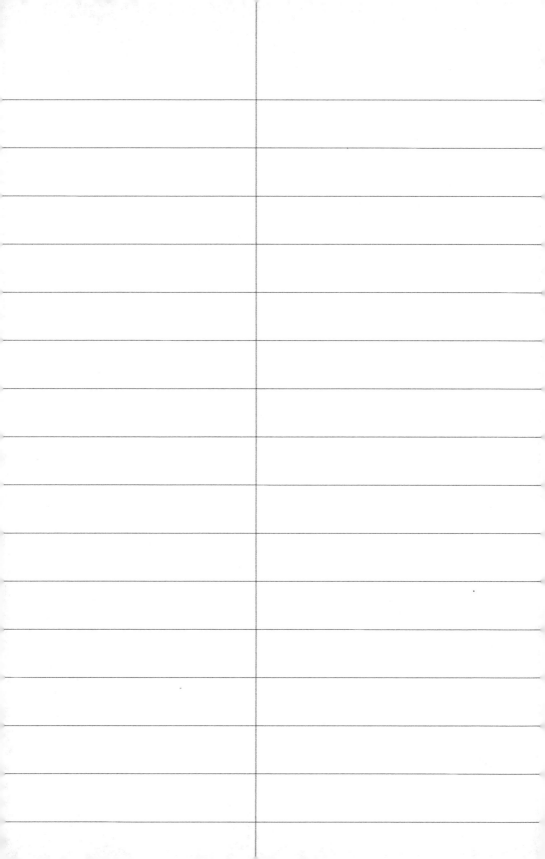

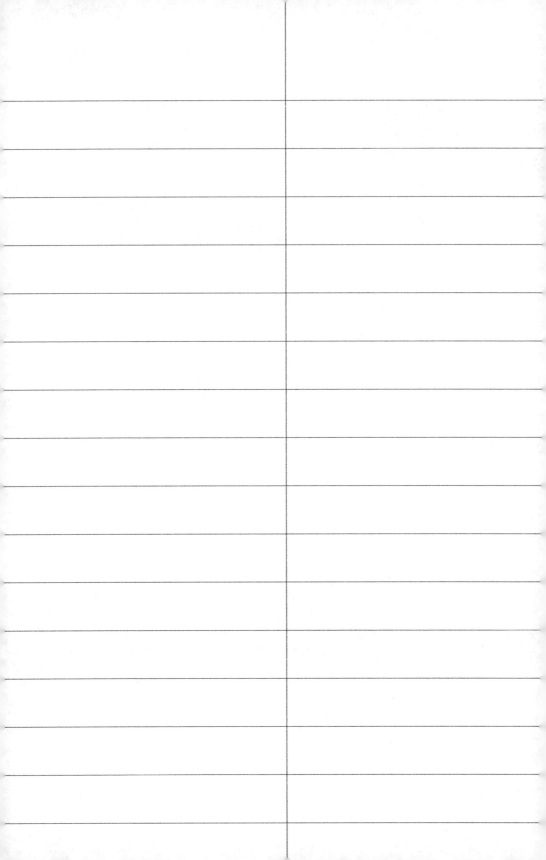

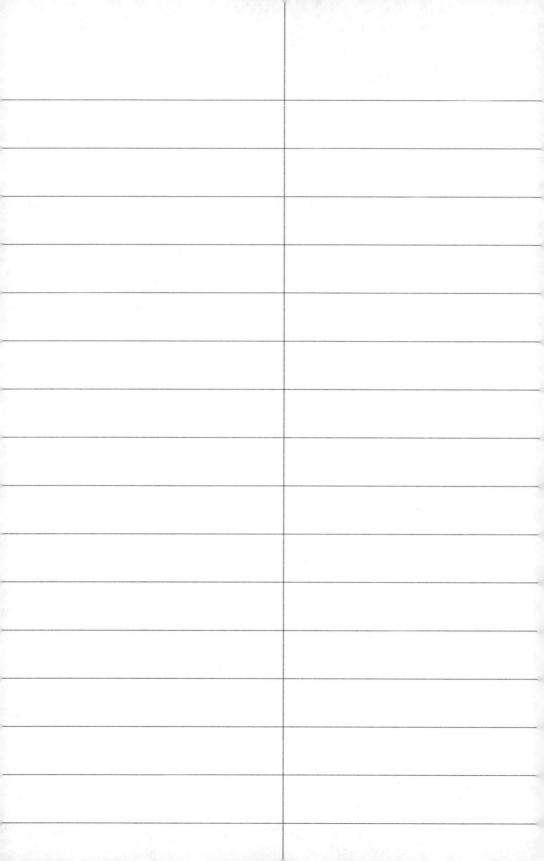

Thank you for buying!

We would like to express our sincerest
gratitude for choosing Pappel 20 products.
Please visit our listing and find more than 20
different types of notebooks.
We appreciate your feedback, please contact us
at Pappel20.Hub@gmail.com

PAPPEL20 TEAM

CPSIA information can be obtained
at www.ICGtesting.com
Printed in the USA
LVHW051259070121
675556LV00004B/579